# TREASURES OF THE BARRIER REEF

by
Geoffrey T. Williams
Illustrated by Pierr Morgan

**PRICE STERN SLOAN**
Los Angeles

Library of Congress Cataloging-in-Publication Data

Williams, Geoffrey T.
Treasures of the barrier reef.

Summary: A young boy and his mother, a marine biologist, have plans for
a quiet vacation on a South Pacific island, but when MURV, a
marine underwater research vehicle. shows up, they go on an expedition
into the strange and beautiful world of the barrier reef.
[1. Underwater exploration—Fiction. 2. Marine biology—Fiction.
3. Islands—Fiction]  I. Morgan, Pierr, ill. II. Title.
PZ7.W65915Tr 1988  [Fic]  87-29211
ISBN 0-8431-1941-1

ISBN: 0-8431-1941-1

For my wife, Dorothea — because of her the sun is bright, the surf is up and I dream Moratonga.

# Treasures Of The Barrier Reef

If you had asked Jon Michaels if he thought this vacation was going to be special, he would have said, "Are you kidding? This is going to be the best one ever!" If you'd asked him why, he'd have said, "Because I've never flown in a jet before. And I've never been farther from home than when we went to Grandma's house in Los Angeles for my tenth birthday last year. And . . ." he'd have said this part with a big grin, ". . . I've never gone diving for treasure before!" Now, here he was at International Airport, getting on an airliner as tall as a three-story building. And here he was with his mother, a marine biologist with the Mid-Ocean Institute, travelling to a place he'd never heard of before, over 8000 miles away from home. And sure enough, here he was, loaded down with fins, a mask and snorkel, off to a South Pacific island where who-knows-what-kind-of-treasure was waiting to be discovered.

"Last call for Flight 441," the public-address announcer called. "All passengers for Tongatapu, Tafahi and Moratonga please board at Gate 12." To Jon, each name sounded full of mystery and adventure.

Jon's mom and dad were talking. "Good luck with the research," his father was saying. Then he turned to Jon. "Oh — and Son? Any treasure you find . . .?"

"I know, Dad. It goes into the bank for college, right?"

His father smiled. "Right." He gave his son a hug, and kissed his wife. "Have a good trip." Then the flight attendant took their boarding passes, and Jon and his mother were on their way.

As the plane lifted off, its giant jet engines rumbled like distant thunder, and Jon closed his eyes, and the sound became the roar of cannons...

The H.M.S. Brigand chased the South Sea pirates through shark-infested waters. Eight-pound cannons roared and thundered. In the middle of the moonless night, the treasure-laden pirate ship slipped away, the skull-and-crossbone flag grinning from the yardarm. But the pirates were helpless in the fury of the howling typhoon. The sixty-knot winds drove them onto the jagged rocks of the hidden reef, tearing the bottom out of the ship. Chests full of gold doubloons and priceless jewelry spilled overboard, sinking out of sight — lost for centuries. Treasure just waiting to be found by the captain of adventure, Jon Michaels. Jon Michaels. Jon...

"Jon," his mother said again.

He opened his eyes. "I...guess I was dreaming, Mom." He rubbed his eyes. "Do you think we'll find any treasure on Moratonga?"

Dr. Dorothea Michaels knew her son's vivid imagination. "There's more treasure than you can imagine waiting on Moratonga. Here's some reading on the island's history." And she held a book out to him.

He took the large, colorful book and opened it up to the first chapter.

## The Birth Of An Island

Deep within the earth is a raging fire. It creates such incredible pressure and heat that solid rock and metal become liquid. This liquid is called "magma." It is the basic building material of the earth, and it surges beneath our planet's crust like a river of lead. The pressure and heat at the earth's core force the magma through hot spots — cracks and rifts — in the crust. More than ten kilometers under the surface of the South Pacific Ocean is a giant rift valley — the vast, underwater formation known as the Tonga Trench.

Millions of years ago the boiling river of magma broke through the Tonga Trench in a series of thunderous explosions that changed the shape of the ocean floor forever. For thousands of years, millions of tons of magma escaped through this hot spot. As it cooled, it became lava, and as layer after layer of lava hardened into rock, a massive underwater volcano was formed. By the end of the earth-age known as the Cretaceous, 60 million years ago, the volcano was taller than any mountain on earth. Its roots were buried deep beneath the sea, and its jagged peak soared thousands of feet into the clouds.

Smoke and steam poured from within the huge crater, and the ground was continually shaking from earthquakes and eruptions.

One day the mountain blew apart. The giant eruption sent rocks and boulders miles into the sky. Shock waves of sound circled the planet. Far away, strange creatures lifted their heads and listened to the echoes of the distant blasts.

The volcano convulsed as the explosions continued to rip it apart. The earth heaved and cracked, sending an avalanche of dirt and rock tumbling down the sides. With a mighty roar, the cone of the mountain collapsed in upon itself, filling the burning crater and smothering the liquid fire deep inside.

For months afterwards, immense clouds of dust and ashes, carried by strong winds, dimmed the light from the sun and fell like dark rain upon the heads of the strange creatures.

Even as the day of the great dinosaurs was coming to an end, the island of Moratonga was born in fire and thunder.

## Living On The Volcano

Jon Michaels compared the violence of the exploding volcano
pictured in the book with the lush, green paradise just outside
— giant ferns, trailing vines and bright flowers grew right up
to the house, and the sounds of tropical birds came in through
the open balcony door.

The house itself was built high on the side of the dormant
volcano. Below was a glittering crescent of sandy beach. The
clear waters of a shallow lagoon, smooth as a tabletop, led out
to a line of waves breaking on the reef a hundred yards off
shore; beyond the reef the deep blue waters of the ocean
stretched to the far horizon.

"That's great!" he heard his mother say. She was sitting at
her desktop computer getting information from the big main-
frame computer at the Mid-Ocean Institute, half a world away,
through a communication satellite up-link.

"What's great, Mom?"

She turned the computer off. "We're having company. The Institute is sending MURV out in a couple of weeks to help me look for hydrothermal vents."

"Who's Murv?"

But she just smiled and said, "It's a surprise. By the way, are you learning much about Moratonga?"

"Yeah. The book's really interesting. But I'd rather see this stuff than just read about it."

"You *will* see it. Just as soon as we've had a chance to do some snorkeling on the reef. Living on Moratonga will be like living in a big oceanographic laboratory."

That sounded exciting. He could start looking for sunken treasure right away. "Can we go now?"

She laughed, "I haven't the faintest idea where my mask and fins are packed. I'll find them tonight and we'll go tomorrow."

A flock of white sea gulls wheeled and cried in the warm, humid air, and the sound of the distant surf was very peaceful. But in his mind, Jon Michaels could still hear echoes of that ancient explosion, and he suspected the waters around Moratonga weren't as peaceful as they looked.

## On The Reef

There was a small rowboat pulled up on the beach below the house.

"We'll anchor it over the reef and use it when we get tired," his mother explained.

"And we'll use it to hold my treasure," the boy thought to himself. Then he asked, "What kind of reef is this?"

"It's called a 'barrier reef' because it forms a barrier between the waves and the island."

"How did it get there?"

"Well, a volcanic island like Moratonga weighs a lot —

billions of tons. So, as soon as the pressures that formed it stopped, the crust supporting the island started sinking back down into the magma."

"You mean the island's sinking right now?" Jon looked around a little nervously.

His mother laughed, "Yes, but don't worry, it takes thousands of years. And as it sinks, wave action grinds boulders into rocks, rocks into pebbles..."

"And pebbles into sand," Jon said, picking up a handful of warm sand and letting it run through his fingers.

"Right," she continued. "Also, rain causes erosion and washes dirt and rocks into the ocean. As the island sinks, a kind of rocky platform is built up around it where the coral can anchor and grow."

"Is coral a plant?"

"Some of it looks like plants, but coral is really a small marine animal — a little like an anemone."

"An animal! I never would have guessed that."

"Colonies of coral attach themselves to the rocky platform around the island. As the old coral dies, the hard calcium skeletons make the foundation for the new coral to grow on."

As they were rowing out to the reef, Jon heard a loud splash.

He looked, and saw a giant creature with wings over twenty feet across leap out and soar over the water for many feet before landing with a sharp "crack" back in the lagoon. "What was that?"

"A manta ray."

"He's beautiful," Jon said, amazed.

As they put on their masks and dropped over the side of the boat into the warm, diamond-bright water of the lagoon, Jon wondered what other surprises were waiting, and just what kind of treasure he might discover.

Moratonga Reef was spread out beneath them. They came up every few minutes so that Jon could ask about the things he was seeing. "That's table coral," his mother told him, pointing to a large, green, flat-topped growth. "And that rounded, soft-looking one is leather coral."

It was so quiet that Jon could hear his breath hiss softly through the snorkel breathing tube. He felt like he was floating through a fantastic underwater garden. He saw delicate branches of staghorn coral, cylinders of tubastrea coral, big boulders of brain coral, lumps of star coral and soft tree coral. There were coral outcroppings in every shape and size as far as he could see. The colors were spectacular. Deep reds, brilliant yellows, somber blues, fragile pinks and every imaginable shade of green. This new underwater world was like nothing he'd ever seen before.

To his surprise, some of the reef's strangest looking, but most beautiful, inhabitants were the worms that anchored on the coral outcroppings. There were colonies of horseshoe worms gently waving in the current, forests of silvery fan worms, tube worms like bright red flowers, cone-shaped Christmas tree worms and fragile featherduster worms.

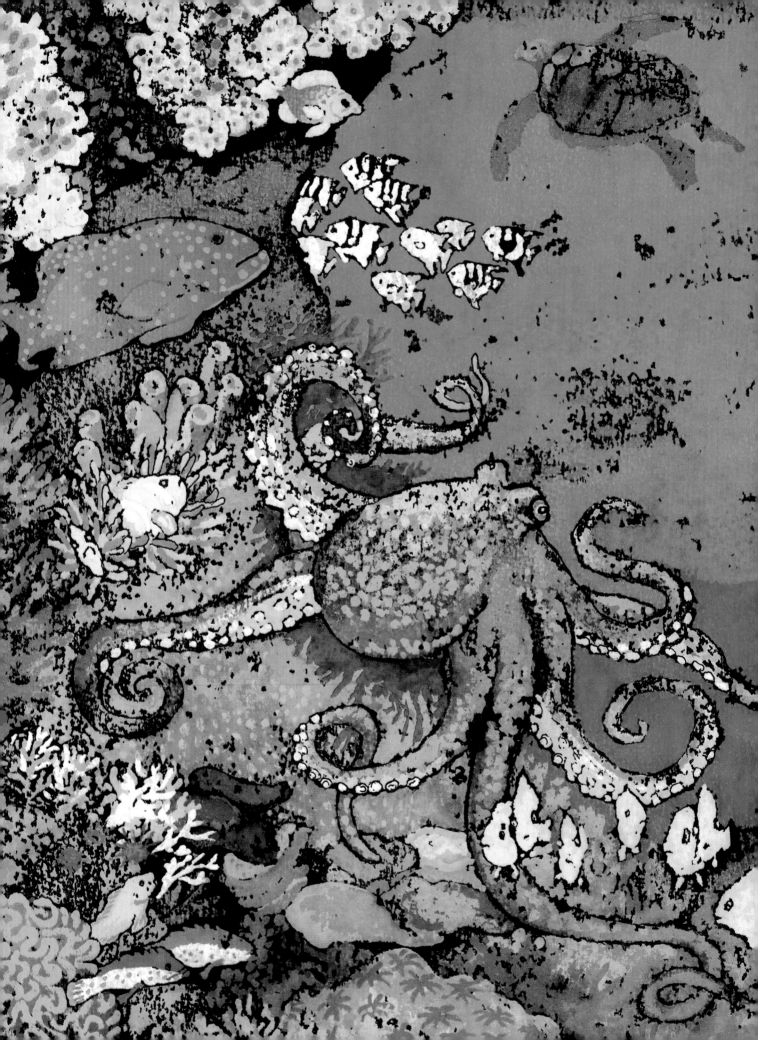

"A coral reef in the sea is like an oasis in the desert," Dr. Michaels told him. "It provides food and protection for an amazing variety of creatures."

Everywhere Jon looked, the reef was teeming with life. In every crack and crevice — swimming, floating and crawling above, around and through the coral — were more fish than he had ever seen in his life.

He watched, fascinated, as an octopus glided by, its eight long tentacles trailing gracefully behind. It was about five feet across, and as it passed, it looked at him with large, round eyes — eyes that seemed to gleam with a purposeful intelligence.

Every day Jon wondered, "Will today be the day I find my treasure?" As they explored the reef, he kept a sharp eye out for the telltale glint of gold and the sparkle of gems.

They saw the octopus often, and Jon was fascinated by how the shy creature pulled itself across the reef — its tentacles moving in complex harmony. Jon nicknamed it "Eight Ball." He began bringing small bits of crabmeat to his "new pet," and one day he was rewarded for his patience when a suckered tentacle reached out and took the food from his hand. Jon was delighted.

"Cephalopods are the most intelligent invertebrates," Jon's mother told him.

"I know an invertebrate is an animal that doesn't have a backbone. But what's a 'cephalopod'?"

"'Cephalopod' means 'head-foot' — an animal whose feet surround its head. Squid and octopuses are cephalopods."

"How big do they get?" Jon wanted to know.

"Octopuses can get up to thirty feet across."

"Thirty feet! That's . . . bigger than our living room!" He tried to imagine feeding a thirty-foot octopus, and had the uncomfortable thought that he might become the meal.

"I don't think we'll run across one that size on Moratonga Reef," his mother said. "In deep water, who knows what we'll discover? But we'll have to wait for MURV to get here to find out."

"I feel like an explorer in another world," Jon told his mother. The eerie blues and greens of the water, the strange shapes of the coral outcroppings and the weird creatures of the sea were almost unearthly. "How do so many different animals get along?"

"'Symbiosis' is the scientific term for the way many of them live together. They help each other. Look at that clown fish."

The brilliantly colored little fish, narrow face as bright as sunlight, was nestled within the purple tentacles of a giant sea anemone, immune to the poisonous sting that would kill other fish.

"It cleans the anemone while the anemone protects it from larger fish with its tentacles. That's an example of a symbiotic relationship. And watch that big grouper," she said as she pointed.

This two-hundred-pound predator could eat dozens of smaller fish at every meal. But now, it was hovering patiently between two coral boulders while bite-size fish called "gobies" swam in and out of its mouth, cleaning off parasites and fungus. Jon even saw a tiny, snack-size shrimp tiptoeing over the body of a seven-foot moray eel, eating the parasites on the skin of the fierce-looking creature, not at all afraid of its razor-sharp teeth.

"There are also 'predator-prey' relationships," his mother told him. "Violence is an everyday fact of life on the reef. Even coral is a predator. It eats microscopic zooplankton that float across the reef."

"But nothing can eat coral, right?" the boy asked.

"Keep your eyes on that blue parrot fish," she told him.

As he watched it grazing over the reef, he realized its special teeth were made just to eat live coral. Suddenly, there was a blur of silver as a barracuda slashed across the reef and grabbed the unsuspecting parrot fish. In one violent instant it was over. One second the parrot fish was a meal for a larger predator. And, Jon realized, even the barracuda was prey to people, who caught and ate or sold it.

"One way or another, I guess everything gets eaten," Jon said.

Once, they came across a small school of leopard sharks. Although Dr. Michaels didn't seem too worried, she did make sure she and Jon stayed a safe distance away. The biggest ones were about six feet long. Jon thought the sleek predators were beautifully colored.

A school of exotically striped fish glided by, and Jon wanted to swim closer for a better look.

"Careful, Jon. Those are lion fish. Their long spines are poisonous to the touch."

"But why?" he wanted to know.

"It's their defense mechanism. Every fish has some kind of defense — speed, size, unusual shape, bad taste, poison or camouflage."

She showed him how a porcupine fish inflates its body until its scales stick out like sharp spikes, making it difficult for other fish to swallow, and how the bizarre, mottled coloring of the scorpion fish helps hide it as it rests on the bottom.

"I'll bet sharks don't need a defense mechanism," he told his mother confidently.

"Yes, they do. Even those leopard sharks have enemies."

"But what could eat them?"

"Bigger sharks" was her answer.

One hot, sunny day as they were snorkeling near Eight Ball's home, Jon noticed some movement by a large boulder of brain coral. As he turned to look, a very strange creature came into view.

From a distance, it appeared to be blue and grey — the color of a shark. It was about shark-size, too: six or seven feet long with a wide, flattened head. It had big, bright eyes and an odd-shaped opening of some kind that might have been a mouth. A long, whiplike tail trailed over the coral behind it. But perhaps the most frightening things were its thick, round arms and strong-looking claws.

Jon hoped the creature wouldn't notice him — but it did, and it began swimming toward him. As the boy backed away, it swam closer, its arms seeming to reach for him. Jon kept moving backward until he bumped into his mother, swimming behind him. The creature surfaced right in front of them, almost close enough to touch. And, to the boy's amazement, it spoke. "Excuse me. Where can I find Dr. Dorothea Michaels?" "Jon," his mother said, "I'd like you to meet MURV."

"MURV stands for Marine Underwater Research Vehicle," Captain Thorne said. "It's a special deep-sea submarine." They were standing on the deck of the "Windhover," anchored in the deep water outside Moratonga Reef. Windhover was the specially equipped "mother ship" that had ferried MURV over to the island from the Mid-Ocean Institute.

"The 'creature' you saw was actually a small robot explorer named 'Aquabot' that I control from inside MURV. I'm sorry if I scared you."

The submersible had been lifted onto the deck of the ship, and the crew was loading supplies into it. Jon could see now that the "eyes" were headlights and the "mouth" was simply the grill over the underwater speaker, while the creature's arms and hands were mechanical limbs used to manipulate objects under water.

MURV was a wonder of high technology. It was built like a big sled, with an eight-foot transparent sphere sitting on top. Mounted on the back of the sled were tanks of air and seawater ballast for diving and surfacing, like a submarine has. There were also fuel cells to power the motors on the front, back and sides and heavy-duty storage batteries used to power the cameras, strobe lights, audio and video tape recorders, and all the other specialized equipment used in deep-sea exploration.

Aquabot had its own batteries, cameras and motors, and rode on a platform in front of MURV when not being used.

"Okay, Captain," Dr. Michaels called. "I think that's everything. Hop in, Jon."

Jon couldn't believe it. "You mean . . . I get to go with you?" he stammered.

"You don't think I brought you halfway around the world just to sit on the beach while I had all the fun, did you?" his mother laughed. "Of course you're coming with us!"

"All right!" Jon shouted.

"How deep are we going to dive?" he asked, as Captain Thorne was closing the hatch over their heads.

"Oh, not more than ten or twelve thousand feet."

"It is dangerous?"

"Well, for every foot under water, pressure increases one pound. At ten thousand feet it's like ten thousand pounds pressing on every square inch of MURV. But he's built to take it." The pressure locks ratcheted into place.

"Don't worry, Jon," his mother said. "Captain Thorne is very experienced, and MURV has been thoroughly tested."

Jon was excited and a little nervous as he settled into the small chair and fastened the seat belt. Dr. Michaels and Captain Thorne began checking equipment, as pilots do before flying. Their voices echoed strangely in the cabin.

"Air pressure?" the captain asked.

"Check," Dr. Michaels answered.

"Robot manipulators?"

"Check."

"Video output?"

"Check."

M.O.I.

As the list went on, Jon looked around the inside of the vehicle that was going to take him thousands of feet below the ocean surface. A lot of the space was taken up by equipment. Video monitors, sonar screens, controls for Aquabot, hand and foot controls for MURV — they were surrounded by switches, buttons, lights, levers, dials, screens, speakers; he wondered how his mother could remember what everything did.

Outside the dome, Jon watched a school of dolphins playfully jumping out of the water and swimming up to within a few feet of the submarine to look curiously at the boy. As they cast off from Windhover and slowly started down to the bottom of the ocean, the dolphins followed along.

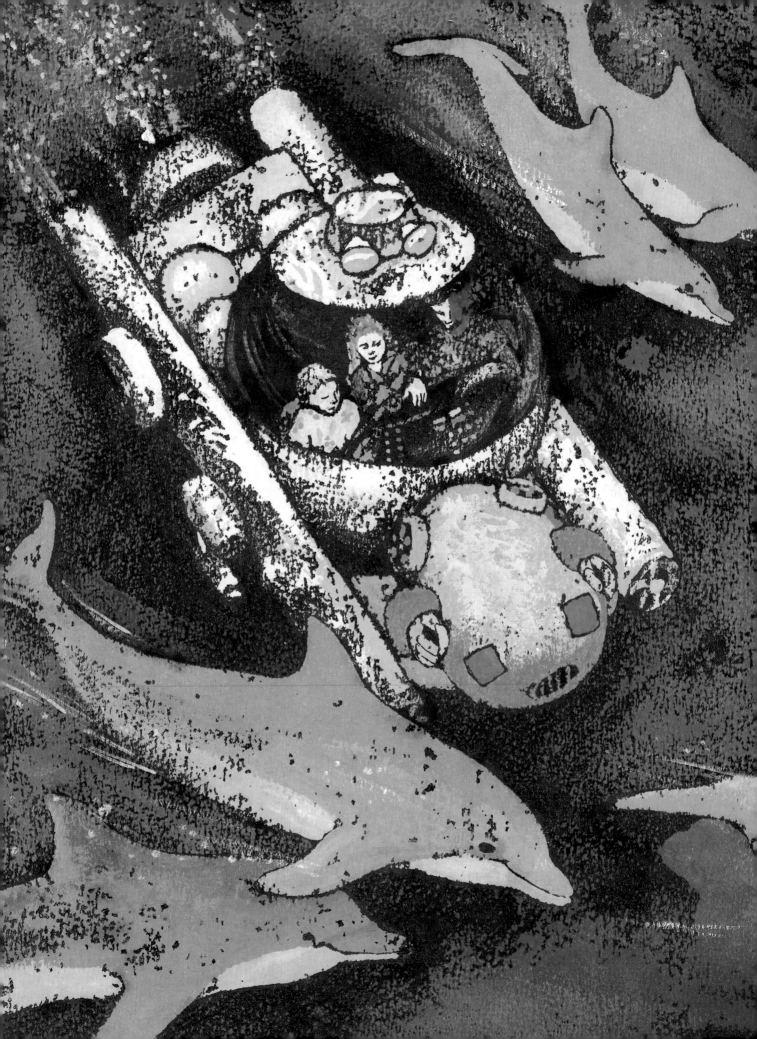

## Into The Deep

The ocean beyond the bubble dome was dark blue and green. Sunlight didn't penetrate very far.

"I can't see much," Jon said. "How do fish live in the dark?"

"They use senses other than sight," his mother answered. "Sharks can detect tiny electric charges emitted by other fish's heartbeats."

"Like an electrocardiogram?" Jon asked.

"Right. And lobsters can taste with their feet and their mouths. And even the sides of some fish are pressure-sensitive, so they can hear with their whole bodies as well as their ears."

"And," Captain Thorne added, "our dolphin friends use echo-location to navigate underwater. Listen."

He turned up the volume on a speaker. A series of high-pitched squeals and clicks sounded in the cabin. "Those sounds they make bounce off objects or fish in the water, and the echoes tell the dolphins how big, what shape and how far away the objects are. This method works the same way sonar does on a submarine."

"But how can we see down here? How do we know where we're going?"

"Just like those dolphins," his mother said, and she flipped a switch. Musical pings filled the cabin. "Our sonar echoes tell us where things are."

Suddenly, the dolphins' squeals got louder and faster.

"The dolphins are sounding a little nervous, Doctor," said Captain Thorne. "We just might have another curious visitor." He flipped a switch on the control console, and the ocean outside was suddenly flooded with light. Jon hardly dared to breathe. He had only seen one in movies before. But now the sleek, grey shape was revealed in all its menace by the sudden brilliance of MURV's powerful strobe lights.

"A great white shark," the boy said in a whisper. The most feared predator in the ocean seemed close enough to touch.

Even Captain Thorne talked more softly. "And a big one, too. Must be twenty-five feet long. And look at those teeth!" The shark opened its mouth, and Jon saw row after row of razor-sharp teeth. "They grow teeth the way you and I grow hair, Jon. They can have over three thousand of them. When one falls out, another one just moves into place."

"It won't come after us, will it?"

"I don't think we look very appetizing to it," Captain Thorne said.

After a brief inspection trip around the submersible, the huge creature dismissed them with a flick of its powerful tail and disappeared into the darkness. Jon gave a sigh of relief. MURV continued deeper.

They came to rest on the ocean bottom where the island of Moratonga rose out of the earth's crust, almost two miles beneath the surface. The only lights were the dim greens and soft reds coming from the instrument panel; the only sounds were the muted "pingings" of the sonar that Captain Thorne was monitoring.

Suddenly, Jon pointed. "What's happening?"

Outside, tiny lights were undulating back and forth, weaving a strange and eerie pattern in the darkness.

"Looks like we've come across some angler fish," Dr. Michaels said. "Watch carefully. I'll turn on the lights and you'll have a few seconds to see them before they swim back into the dark. Ready?"

Nothing could have made him ready for what he saw next. In his worst nightmare, Jon could never have imagined creatures like these. Gaping jaws. Long, needle-thin teeth. Round, beady eyes. Slick, dark skin with no scales. And, weirdest of all, each angler fish had a growth on the front of its upper jaw — the source for the lights the boy had seen.

On one fish the growth was like a piece of seaweed. On another, it was a tiny luminescent bulb on the end of a long, whiplike stem. One fish had a beard of fleshy, finger shapes hanging from its chin which seemed to crawl with a life of their own.

"What are those?"

"Fishing lures."

"You mean those fish *fish*?"

"That's right. They wave their lures around and, in the darkness, smaller fish think it's food, so they chase it. Right into the angler's mouth."

"But how do the lures shine?"

"'Bioluminescence.' A chemical reaction — the same kind that makes fireflies glow."

The sub's bright lights disturbed the bizarre fish, and in a few moments they had all disappeared. But in the dark ocean beyond the submarine, Jon saw dim pinpoints of light begin to dance and weave slow patterns once more as the anglers continued their strange feeding ritual.

"What are we trying to find down here?" the boy asked.

His mother looked up from writing instrument readings in the submarine logbook. "'Black smokers.' That's what scientists call the hydrothermal vents where super-heated seawater is forced back out into the ocean from cracks in the earth's crust."

"Why are they important?"

"The Mid-Ocean Institute sent me over here to try and find out if Moratonga was becoming an active volcano again. One sign would be black smokers on the ocean floor."

The bottom was a rugged jungle of jagged lava boulders. Using the hydrophone to listen to the sounds from the ocean outside, they began the search. Jon became aware of a distant sound, like water shooting out of a hose. "Listen," he told them.

Dr. Michaels said quietly, "You've got good ears, Jon. I hear it now, too. Five degrees right rudder."

"There!" said the boy. "Just ahead."

At the edge of the light, Jon pointed to what appeared to be darker water.

The sound was much louder now, and Captain Thorne slowed MURV almost to a standstill. The strobe lights fought to penetrate the inky blackness.

As MURV got closer and Jon was able to see better, he asked his mother how it was possible for black smoke to be rising from the ocean floor.

"It's not really smoke, Jon. Chemicals in the hot water, mostly sulphides, give it that color."

Captain Thorne was examining the rocks ahead. "It's too small for MURV to get in there. We'll have to send Aquabot."

Hydraulic systems whined and servo-motors hummed as the small explorer robot came to life. TV screens inside MURV flickered and brightened as the probe's lights came on and its cameras powered up.

''Everything that Aquabot sees, we'll see too, Jon,'' the captain said. Then he launched the robot explorer toward the smoky blackness ahead, guiding it with the hand controls on MURV's console.

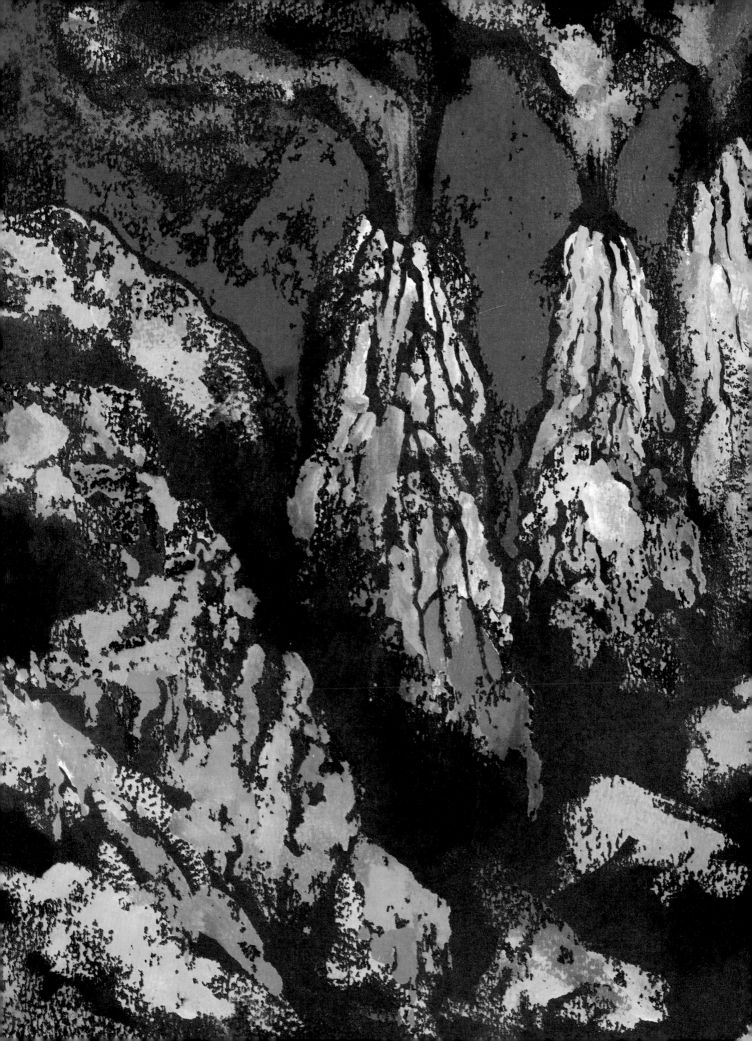

## Halloween

Aquabot glided toward the source of the black smoker, the control cable trailing out behind. With the cameras mounted on all sides of the robot, Captain Thorne was able to monitor every movement, and guide the craft almost as easily as driving a car or flying a plane. He slowed down where a cloud of black water streamed from between jagged boulders.

The noise of the rushing water thundered in the speakers. Dr. Michaels turned it down. The dark water obscured the camera's view, but Captain Thorne had done this kind of thing before. He nudged the control lever, and dropped the robot down until it was below the cloud of water. Chemical deposits had built up a weird, rough chimney-like mound. A jet black stream of water, thick as a tree trunk, gushed out. The boy couldn't take his eyes off the TV screens. The world around the hydrothermal vent was so strange it was almost unimaginable.

Here, miles beneath the ocean's surface, was a world of Halloween colors and freakish creatures. The chemicals carried up from beneath the earth's crust by the hot water colored the rocks orange, black, yellow, brown and red.

As Aquabot turned its cameras, Jon pointed at something in the picture. "What are those?"

"Vent worms," the captain told him.

They sprouted between the rocks around the vent like giant grass, weaving and turning in the currents. The longest was two or three meters — over ten feet long — and as thick as a garden hose.

"How can worms get that big?"

His mother was taking notes on everything the cameras showed. She wrote as she answered, "That water is 300 to 400 degrees Celsius — three or four times hotter than boiling water. Within a few meters of the vent, it's warm enough and rich enough in minerals to help things grow in ways we don't fully understand yet."

"We know one thing," put in Captain Thorne. "It helps them grow big. Look at those clams."

"They're as big as dinner plates!" Jon exclaimed.

"A normal clam wouldn't get that big in ten years. Down here there's so much food that they grow that big in just two or three years." Then, using the control handles, Captain Thorne activated Aquabot's manipulators. On the screen, they watched the mechanical arms reach out and delicately pick up one of the huge clams and tuck it in a carrying bag.

During the slow trip back to the surface, Dr. Michaels was taking more notes. Captain Thorne was piloting MURV, and Jon was watching the radar screen and listening to the hydrophone.

They got to within a quarter of a mile of the surface when he noticed something unusual. "What is that?"

His mother looked at the screen, then at the captain. "Unidentified object approaching. One hundred yards off the port side." She sounded concerned.

So did Captain Thorne. "I'm going to stop until we find out what it is." MURV's motors wound down. They were now floating motionless.

"Twenty-five yards," Jon's mother said quietly. "Whatever it is — it's big. Fifty, maybe sixty feet long. And it's headed straight for us . . . it's stopped now . . . about ten meters dead ahead."

"I think it's time to shed some light on our visitor," Captain Thorne said, and reached for the strobe light switch.

Again, the dark ocean outside the dome was flooded with brilliant light. Outlined in the brightness was an awesome sight.

"I've never seen one that big," the captain breathed.

"Does MURV have any defenses against it?" Dr. Michaels asked.

"Not really. Look at those tentacles. They're as big around as tree trunks."

"Isn't that a giant squid?" Jon asked nervously.

"That's right. I don't think we have anything to worry about. But you never can . . ."

"Here it comes!" interrupted Dr. Michaels. A huge tentacle reached out and rested on the front of MURV, right next to Aquabot. "Maybe that clam we picked up is attracting it."

Suddenly, the submarine lurched as the squid yanked at the clam shell. Jon could see the creature's sharp beak opening and closing hungrily. Its basketball-size eyes gazed, unblinking, at the trio of humans in the submersible. Jon was starting to worry. But just then, a strange sound filled the cabin — low moaning tones, almost below the human threshold of hearing. Then, high, soaring bursts of sound — abrupt yips and piercing squeals. It built to a crescendo as first one, and then many, voices joined the first. Jon had never heard anything like it before. It was a sound as ancient as the ocean and hauntingly beautiful.

"The humpback whales," his mother said.

"It . . . it sounds like they're singing," Jon whispered.

"They are singing," she told him. "And look!"

Outside, the giant squid had let loose of the submarine and was nervously withdrawing back into the darkness, beyond the lights. As the squid disappeared, huge, shadowy shapes came into view. Jon held his breath as the whales swam by.

"They know we're here," said the captain. "They're looking right at us."

Their massive bodies, several over sixty feet long, moved with unmistakable power, yet these huge creatures had an almost delicate grace. Their long flippers were edged with white and gleamed in the dark blue of the water. Their tail flukes surged rhythmically. Each whale gazed at the submersible as it passed, large eyes bright with intelligence.

"Why are they singing?" the boy asked.

"It's the solitary males that sing, perhaps looking for mates. We're very close to their breeding grounds."

As the whales passed, they sang. Jon thought he had never heard any sound so strange and unearthly — and at the same time, so beautiful.

MURV surfaced close to the Windhover, and soon they were all gathered on the deck of the mother ship, safe and sound after their voyage to the bottom of the sea.

Jon's mother was making some final notations in her logbook when she heard a distant noise and glanced up. "Well, it looks like some of our questions about Moratonga have been answered, Jon."

He followed her gaze to the top of the steep mountain and saw a wisp of black smoke curl from the peak. The mountain gave an almost imperceptible shudder. Moratonga was coming back to life.

Jon had grown used to the sound of waves gently slapping the sand and the faraway cries of sea gulls. He thought the airport was crowded and noisy. But still, he was glad to be home. There was a big family hug when his father met them, followed by lots of smiles, questions and stories. On the way home Jon's father asked, "So tell me, Son, did you find the treasure you were looking for?"

Jon thought awhile, about the diamond-bright sands along Moratonga Lagoon, the quicksilver flash of the barracuda, the ruby red fire that the mountain held like a precious secret deep inside, the sapphire blue waters of the reef, the emerald green and aquamarine of the coral, the golden glow of the sun slipping into the sea at the end of each day.

Jon thought about these things and smiled. "I guess I did, Dad. I guess I found my treasure after all."